QUIET MY HEART : 31 DAYS OF ENCOURAGEMENT FOR MOTHERS

DAILY DEVOTIONS TO REMIND YOU YOU'RE SEEN, KNOWN AND DEEPLY LOVED

EVELYN HOPE

CONTENTS

Disclaimer: The devotional readings in this book are creative reflections written in the style of personal letters. While they are inspired by themes and truths found in the Bible, they represent one woman's personal interpretation and experience of God's Word. They are not the actual words of God, nor should they be considered equivalent to Scripture.

The intent is to encourage readers in their faith and to point them back to the authority of God's Word — *and to the loving heart of the One who wrote it.*

WELCOME

Do you sometimes feel like you give and give until there's nothing left? Or perhaps you lie awake at night wondering if you're enough?

Does it ever seem like all the quiet, hidden things you do for everyone else go unseen and unappreciated?

This book is for the mother who loves so fiercely it sometimes hurts - and for the woman beneath all the roles you carry.

It isn't about trying harder or becoming a better mom. It's an invitation to *pause. To breathe.*

To hear God speak to your heart, right where you are - the real you.

Maybe someone who loves you placed it in your hands, knowing you needed to hear what's written here.

Or maybe you picked it up yourself in a quiet moment, hoping for something - anything - to reach the bone-tired parts of you that long for *rest, for hope, for a reminder that you're not alone.*

These pages are written as *letters from God's heart to yours.*

Whether you read one devotion a day or steal a few moments whenever you can, I pray this little book reminds you of what's true:

You are seen. You are deeply loved. And you are so, so precious to your Heavenly Father.

Blessings,

Evelyn

ONE
YOU ARE CHOSEN

"Before I formed you in the womb I knew you,
before you were born I set you apart."

- JEREMIAH 1:5 (NIV)

My beautiful daughter,

Before time began, I knew you.

Before you held your child, I held you.

I chose you.

You are not an accident. Not a mistake.

I planned you and appointed you, with love.

Your calling as a mother isn't something you achieve - it's something you receive.

You don't have to earn your place. You don't have to prove your worth through performance.

Because, You are My daughter - loved beyond measure and chosen beyond doubt.

You are walking in a divine calling.

Each child a gift, placed in your life because I knew exactly what they would need. They need you.

Not the "perfect" version of you. Not the one who never raises her voice or who has a perfect home.

Just you. The real you. The one I created, the one I delight in.

So let go of the pressure, the expectations and the fears that you're not enough.

Breathe deep.

Give Me those things you don't yet understand.

Trust Me with the parts of motherhood that stretch you.

I will give you exactly what you need for each day.

I will lead and guide you, if you lean in and listen for My voice.

And on the days when it all feels like too much, come back to this truth:

You were chosen. You are still chosen.

I've never asked or expected you to be perfect.

I'm simply inviting you to let Me carry the load.

Invite Me into your day.

TWO
YOU ARE FULLY KNOWN AND DEEPLY LOVED

"You have searched me, Lord, and you know me."

PSALM 139:1-4 (NIV)

My precious one,

I know you. Every part of you.

I know what makes you laugh and I know what stirs your fears.

I know your thoughts, your hopes, your dreams and your fears.

I know every part of your story - the joys, the shame and the pain.

I know when you're questioning your ability and when you're doubting your worth.

I know the places in your heart you haven't shared with anyone else.

And I love you. Fully. Completely. Without condition or hesitation.

There is nothing hidden from Me. And still, you are My delight.

You are never too much, never too little.

You never have to hide from Me, or pretend to be something you're not. I see every high, every low, every struggle - and I'm here for you.

Nothing can ever change My love for you.

Let this truth settle in your soul today.

You are Mine.

You are My beloved and I cherish you.

You are fully known - and you are deeply, eternally loved.

Always.

THREE
YOU ARE SEEN

*"Can a mother forget the baby at her breast
and have no compassion on the child she has
borne? Though she may forget, I will not
forget you! See, I have engraved you on the
palms of my hands .."*

ISAIAH 49:15-16 (NIV)

My Beloved Daughter,

I see you.

You may feel unseen in the ordinary, unnoticed in the daily rhythm of loving, giving, guiding, comforting, and holding it all together.

But I see you. I am there in all of it.

I see the quiet love behind your choices. I see the weight you carry, even when you don't speak it out loud.

When the world rushes by, when no one notices the effort you give or the strength it takes to simply keep going-I do.

You are not invisible to Me.

I see the questions you hold in your heart. I know the pressure you carry to be everything for everyone. I hear the doubt that whispers, "Am I enough? Does this matter?"

And I want to answer with a resounding *yes*!

You matter. Every act of love matters. Every time you show up - tired, stretched thin - and choose to keep going, it matters.

The world may not notice. People may forget. But I see it all.

So come close to Me. Rest your heart in Mine. Let Me carry what you're holding.

Let Me remind you, again, that you are *seen*.

Lift your eyes, my beloved. You are never out of My sight.

Do you know how close you are to Me? I engraved you on the palms of My hands. That's how treasured, how permanent, how precious you are.

But before you were anything to anyone else, you were Mine.

I didn't choose you because of what you could do. I chose you because of who you are.

My daughter. My delight. My beloved.

That hasn't changed and it never will.

FOUR
YOU ARE HELD BY MY LOVE

"The faithful love of the Lord never ends! His mercies never cease. Great is his faithfulness.."

LAMENTATIONS 3:22–23 (NLT)

My child,

I make each day just for you and I go ahead of you into each moment, and offer fresh strength, wisdom, and mercy.

My love for you never runs dry.

My kindness toward you never ends.

Every morning, I offer a brand-new supply of what your heart, body and spirit need.

Not recycled. Not leftovers.

Fresh new power and strength for each day.

Every day is a new beginning, a blank page to write on.

You don't need to have everything mapped out. You only need to begin each day with Me.

Let go of the pressure to do it all.

Let go of your fears about what tomorrow might bring.

Tomorrow isn't yours yet. It's Mine. And I'm not asking you to live in what hasn't happened.

I'm right here - in this day with you.

So, don't worry about tomorrow. Tomorrow will take care of itself.

Let today be enough.

Let Me be enough for today.

Take a moment to ask Me for what you need.

I will meet you there.

Peace isn't found in having it all figured out.

It's found in walking through your day with Me.

So take a breath. You don't need to have the answers. You don't need to do it perfectly.

Let's begin each day together.

With you holding on to Me, and Me holding you steady through each moment.

FIVE
YOU ARE MY DELIGHT

*"For the Lord your God is living among you. He
is a mighty Savior. He will take delight in
you with gladness. With His love, He will
calm all your fears."*

- ZEPHANIAH 3:17 (NLT)

My beautiful child,

I want you to hear something simple and true today:

I delight in you.

Not in what you accomplish, not only when you feel strong or
confident or capable - I delight in you today and every day.

In every season, in every moment - even the hard ones - this
remains true.

You are more cherished than you realise, more precious than you know.

I delight in your voice, in your heart, in the way you care and the way you carry so much love inside you.

I take such joy in you, and who you are becoming.

You don't have to work for My attention. You already have it. You don't have to earn My affection - it's yours freely, forever.

When I look at you, I don't see a list of things to fix. I see my beloved daughter who makes Me smile.

I see your struggle - but I also see your courage.

I see your weaknesses - but I also see your strengths.

I know the pressures you face - but I also see your beauty in the middle of it.

I rejoice over you. I sing over your life with joy.

So, let My love quiet your heart.

Let My presence give you rest.

Let My Spirit comfort you.

I made you. I chose you.

So rest in this truth: You are My delight - not just today, but always.

SIX
YOU ARE CARRIED

"Even to your old age and gray hairs I am he, I am he who will sustain you. I have made you and I will carry you; I will sustain you and I will rescue you."

ISAIAH 46:4 (NIV)

My precious one,

I know the burdens you carry, your responsibilities, your worries. I see the silent strength you summon just to keep going.

And I want you to hear this clearly today:

You are not alone in this. I am carrying you.

Don't feel as if you have to carry everything alone.

Even when you feel like the weight of the day is yours to hold - I'm already holding you.

I have carried you since the very beginning, since your first breath, your first steps, every first, I have been with you. I've been with you through every season.

There is no moment of your life that is too messy, too hard, or too difficult for Me to carry you through.

You don't need to hold it all together.

I am strong enough to carry both you and everything that concerns you.

You don't have to keep striving to hold it all together or prove you're strong. Not to Me, not to anyone else.

Strength is not something I ask for - it's something I *give*.

So come - even if you're tired. Even if you're unsure. Even if you don't have the words.

Let Me carry you.

Not just when things are hard, but every day.

I will carry you through every season—from this moment to your very last breath.

You were never meant to do this alone.

So let go of the burdens you've been holding.

I've got you.

And I'm not letting go.

SEVEN
YOU ARE ENOUGH

"But he said to me, 'My grace is sufficient for you, for my power is made perfect in weakness.'"

2 CORINTHIANS 12:9 (NIV)

Precious child,

You are enough—not because of all you do, but because of who I am in you.

But here is what I want you to know:

With Me, *you have enough because you are held by the One who is enough.*

My grace is sufficient. And that means you are too.

I know you feel the weight of "not enough" pressing on you.

Not enough time. Not enough patience. Not enough energy.

But I've never asked you to be limitless—I've asked you to rely on Me.

My grace is not a backup plan for when you run out. It's a steady stream that can carry you from moment to moment, breath by breath.

You don't need to strive to measure up or prove your worth.

You're not being tested—you're being loved.

You are not lacking. You are not behind. You are held by the One who is always enough.

So when the whisper comes: "You're not enough"—

Remember whose you are.

My grace fills every gap.

Where you are weak, I am strong.

You don't have to be perfect. You just have to be Mine.

And you are.

Stop measuring.

Stop comparing.

I'm not asking you for more.

I'm simply asking you to receive what I'm already giving:

My presence. My enough-ness living in you.

That's what makes you enough.

EIGHT
YOU WERE MADE FOR THIS MOMENT

"Perhaps you were made for just such a time as this."

- ESTHER 4:14 (ADAPTED)

My Daughter,

You may not always feel ready.

You may wonder if someone else could do this better.

You may wish you had more patience, more wisdom, more strength.

But I want you to hear Me clearly:

I made you for this moment.

Every season you walk through, every lesson, every quiet stretch of waiting - it's all shaping you. I am building wisdom in you. I am growing strength.

What you face today, you don't face alone. I am with you, guiding and forming you. I will give you what you need, when you need it.

You don't need to rush or try to figure it all out. You simply need to lean in.

Listen for My voice in the small moments. Pay attention to the quiet invitations to pause, to pray, to rest.

Even the things you struggle with play a part in how I am shaping you.

You may not feel ready for every step, but that's not your burden to carry.

I am making you ready for all that you'll face. I will give you everything you need.

So let Me lead you. Let Me strengthen you.

Let Me continue the work I've started in you.

You may not know what tomorrow holds, but I do - and I am preparing you for it.

I will show you how to love with My love, lead with My peace, and walk in step with My wisdom.

Walk with Me today. I am preparing you for the days ahead - one step, one day, one moment at a time.

NINE
YOU ARE SAFE TO LET GO

"Trust in the Lord with all your heart and lean not on your own understanding; in all your ways submit to him, and he will make your paths straight."

- PROVERBS 3:5-6 (NIV)

Precious child,

You don't have to carry it all.

You don't have to hold everything so tightly.

You are safe to let go.

To trust Me instead of trying to control everything.

I am here.

I'm inviting you to trust.

To rest instead of striving.

To release, instead of holding on.

So, let go of the fears that whisper into your peace.

Let go of the pressure to control.

Let go of the anger and the worry.

Let go of the comparison, of the pressure to be "enough."

I see what you've been carrying.

Give it to me.

Let Me guide your steps.

Let Me carry what you were never meant to hold.

Trust isn't about having all the answers - it's about knowing who I am.

And I am faithful, loving and present.

Every detail of your life matters to Me.

Nothing is too small for My care.

Nothing is too heavy for Me to carry.

So, come close.

Open your hands.

Place your cares and worries in My hands.

I am strong enough to hold them all.

TEN

YOU ARE HELD IN EVERY TOMORROW

"The Lord Himself goes before you and will be with you; He will never leave you nor forsake you."

- DEUTERONOMY 31:8 (NIV)

Dear Daughter,

I see your quiet fears about the future - the questions you don't always ask out loud.

You may wonder what's coming, whether you'll be ready, whether you'll have the strength.

You reach into tomorrow and carry the weight of what hasn't happened yet.

But I want you to know: *I'm already there.*

I'm already in every tomorrow.

Before a single moment unfolds, I've gone ahead.

I see the road you can't yet see.

I know the outcomes you can't predict.

And I've already prepared what you'll need.

There's grace waiting for you in every tomorrow - grace for what's changing, grace for what stays hard, and grace for the things you haven't seen coming.

You don't have to have it all figured out.

You just need to stay close.

I've gone ahead to prepare the way, and I'll be right beside you through each step.

There's no place you'll ever go that I haven't already made room for you in.

No moment will ever catch Me off guard.

And no day will ever come without Me there to meet you.

So breathe. Rest. Lift your eyes.

When you're walking with Me, you are not walking into uncertainty.

I hold your future as surely as I hold your hand.

You are safe, because I will never leave your side.

ELEVEN
YOU ARE NEVER ALONE

"The Lord himself goes before you and will be with you; he will never leave you nor forsake you..."

DEUTERONOMY 31:8 (ADAPTED FROM NLT)

My Daughter,

This is My promise to you - I will never leave you.

I will never abandon you.

I will never give up on you.

I am with you - always.

I'm here when you rise in the morning.

I'm near when you pause in the middle of your day.

I'm with you when you lie down at night.

Every moment that feels uncertain, I've already seen.

Every place your feet take you, I've already gone ahead.

Let My presence be your strength.

My presence doesn't depend on how you feel.

I am the constant in every season.

You are never out of My reach.

I go before you to prepare the way, and I stay beside you to carry the weight.

You are never alone.

I'm with you in the busyness and in the quiet.

I'm with you when you feel strong, and I'm with you when you feel unsure.

I'm with you in the darkest valleys and I'm with you on the mountaintops.

Whatever happens, I will never leave you.

Never.

TWELVE
YOU ARE HEARD

"The righteous cry out, and the Lord hears them; he delivers them from all their troubles."

- PSALM 34:17 (NIV)

My Daughter,

I hear you.

Before the words leave your lips - I hear.

Before your tears fall - I know.

Before you even realize what your heart is asking - I am already listening.

I hear every tear.

Every sigh is a prayer.

You never need to come to Me with polished prayers or perfect phrases.

You only need to come - just as you are.

Even if all you bring are your tears.

Even if all you bring is a whispered hope or a cry in the darkness.

I am always there, ready to listen.

I hear every word, every emotion, and hold them with care.

This is My promise to you:

When you call to Me, I will draw near.

When you have no words, I will hear what you cannot express.

When you weep, I will weep with you.

When you open your heart, I will come close.

I will never grow tired of your prayers.

I will never turn away from you.

I will never stop listening—or stop loving the sound of your voice turned toward Me.

You are always heard.

Always known. Always loved.

So come to Me, again and again, not because you must, but because you can.

I am here. And I will always hear you.

THIRTEEN
YOU ARE FREE FROM CONDEMNATION

"Therefore, there is now no condemnation for those who are in Christ Jesus."

- ROMANS 8:1 (NIV)

My Precious Child,

I created you to live free - free from shame, free from fear, free from trying to earn what I've freely given to you.

As My child, you are covered by My grace.

There is no condemnation - not today, not ever.

I have thrown your sins into the deepest ocean and spoken freedom over your life. I have declared you clean, whole, and fully accepted.

The guilt you carry? I already carried it for you.

The shame that whispers you're not enough? I've silenced it with My love.

The fear that you'll never measure up? I've replaced it with My grace.

Now I'm inviting you to walk forward in *freedom*.

Where you once carried guilt and shame, now you can carry peace.

Where you once lived striving, now you can live loved.

You don't have to prove yourself to anyone.

You don't have to earn what's already yours.

You have been set free.

Free from condemnation.

Free to breathe. Free to rest. Free to be Mine.

Let Me be your confidence.

Let My truth be louder than the voice that says you're not enough.

Let My presence remind you that you are already loved, already chosen, already free.

Nothing can take away My gift of grace.

So lift your head today.

Walk without fear.

This is the life I've given you: a life of freedom.

Come, receive it. Live in it. Walk in it with Me.

FOURTEEN
YOU ARE DOING HOLY WORK

"Let us not become weary in doing good, for at the proper time we will reap a harvest if we do not give up."

GALATIANS 6:9 (NIV)

Cherished One,

What you do today matters.

Even when it feels small. Even when it feels repetitive.

Every act of love, every word of truth, every moment of quiet faithfulness, this is your holy calling.

You are a vessel of grace, carrying My love into the everyday.

You are a reflection of My faithfulness in a world that desperately needs it.

Nothing you do in love is ever wasted.

I see your effort.

I see your heart.

And I am at work in it all.

You are sowing seeds - seeds that will bloom in their season.

Not today, perhaps. Not even tomorrow.

But in the right time, at the perfect moment, you will see the harvest.

So keep sowing.

Let Me water what you plant.

Trust Me to bring the harvest.

Let My Spirit breathe fresh purpose into your days.

Let joy rise again.

This is kingdom work you are doing - and it has eternal value.

So, lift your head.

You are not laboring in vain.

You are doing work that will echo in eternity.

I am with you in every step, every moment, every season.

FIFTEEN
YOU ARE TREASURED

"You are precious to me. You are honored, and I love you."

ISAIAH 43:4 (ADAPTED)

My precious child,

You are treasured.

Right here, right now.

Not when you achieve something.

Not because you do something.

Not because you earn it or have it all together.

But because you are My daughter.

This is a truth I want you to hold on to:

Your worth is not measured by what you accomplish, but by My love for you.

And that love is as endless as the oceans, as steady as the rising sun, as constant as the stars I set in place.

It does not fade with time. It does not waver with circumstances.

For I am the same yesterday, today, and forever.

My love for you will never run dry — nothing can break it, nothing can stop it.

My love surrounds you when you are still, and it carries you when you feel weary.

As surely as the waves reach the shore, My love will always reach you.

As surely as the morning breaks through the night, My love will always find you.

And as surely as the stars light the heavens above, I will always love you.

For you are My beloved.

You are My delight.

You are more valuable than gold and more radiant than jewels.

You are My treasure — now and for all eternity.

SIXTEEN
YOU ARE IN THE POTTER'S HANDS

"We are the clay, and you are the potter. We all are formed by your hand."

ISAIAH 64:8 (NLT)

My Daughter,

You pour so much of yourself into helping others - watching them learn, stretch, and grow into who they're becoming.

And just as you are watching them, I am gently watching you.

I see who you are becoming and you bring Me such joy.

I see the strength that's being built quietly.

I see your wisdom growing, as your trust in Me grows.

I see the struggles you face and the hurt you carry.

And I know it's hard.

But I can use even these things to shape you.

I'm not wasting any of it—every moment of stretching and gentle pressure can help shape you into the woman I created you to be.

I can use every season — even the hard ones — to shape something beautiful and strong.

You don't need to see the full design yet. You don't need to understand every turn of the wheel.

Just stay soft in My hands.

I will never shape you beyond what you can bear.

Trust the process. Trust Me.

I am the Potter, and you are the clay.

I've started something good in you, and I am still at work— lovingly and faithfully shaping you.

You are becoming the masterpiece I always saw in you.

You don't need to strive. You don't need to compare yourself with others or question if you're doing enough.

Just keep walking with Me.

Let Me continue shaping you, day by day.

What I'm creating in you is more beautiful than you can imagine.

You are becoming exactly what I intended: a vessel of My love and strength.

SEVENTEEN
YOU ARE HELD

"He is before all things, and in Him all things hold together."

COLOSSIANS 1:17 (NIV)

My Chosen One,

I am the One who holds *all* things - and that includes you.

I hold your mind, your heart, your hopes, your family, your future.

I hold every part of it in My hands.

And I'm not letting go.

So, don't feel you have to 'hold it all together'. That's My job.

I invite you to rest in My strength.

Even when you feel frayed at the edges, I am the One who holds you and all those you love.

I hold you - all of you - together. Now and every day.

As you have held your children close, so I hold you even closer.

So, release your cares into My hands.

Stop trying to hold it all together.

Let Me hold you.

Bring Me your worries and your fears.

Give Me your heavy burdens.

Let Me carry what you cannot.

Just give them to Me and let go.

And come, just as you are.

Not with polished answers or a put-together life.

Just you.

My beloved daughter, carried and always held in My arms.

Rest in this truth:

You are not alone.

Your name is engraved in the palms of My hands.

And you are held in My heart - now and always.

EIGHTEEN
YOU ARE INVITED TO REST

*"Come to me, all you who are weary and
burdened, and I will give you rest."*

MATTHEW 11:28 (NIV)

My cherished one,

This is an invitation to you.

An invitation to rest.

You don't have to hold everything together.

You don't have to push through or prove anything to Me.

You simply need to rest.

Rest in Me.

When you're tired, stretched, or overwhelmed, come to Me. Just as you are.

You don't need the right words.

You don't need to have it all figured out.

Simply come.

I'm already here, waiting for you.

Let Me be your place of rest.

Let Me carry what's heavy.

Let Me remind you that your true worth is in who you are to Me:

My daughter.

Loved. Safe. Carried.

With Me, there's grace for each moment and strength for the next.

There's no judgment.

Just love.

Just Me.

So take a breath.

Lean in.

Let go of the pressure.

Let go of the to-do list.

Let Me hold it all.

And come rest with Me.

NINETEEN
YOU ARE PART OF A BIGGER STORY

"For we are God's masterpiece. He has created us anew in Christ Jesus, so we can do the good things He planned for us long ago."

- EPHESIANS 2:10 (NLT)

My beloved daughter,

You are part of a bigger story than you can imagine. My story.

Your thread connects to countless others - women who have walked before you, those walking alongside you now, and those who will follow.

Every act of love you offer, every prayer you whisper, every moment of faithfulness ripples outward.

You may not see the full picture yet, but I do.

Trust Me.

I am weaving something beautiful and lasting.

Your life has purpose, even on those days when what you do feels unseen or unappreciated.

The work of your hands, the words you speak, the kindness you carry - it all matters.

The choices you make with your quiet faithfulness, the love you give without applause, the courage you show in ordinary moments - each of these is a precious thread in the masterpiece I am weaving.

So walk with Me.

Trust that I have prepared good things for you.

Trust that your part - even when it feels small - is significant. It has deep meaning.

Nothing is wasted. Nothing is missed.

You are part of My bigger story and purpose.

And when you can't see how it all fits, trust that I, the Master Weaver do.

Keep showing up. Keep saying yes. Keep leaning in.

Your story matters - because it is woven into Mine.

TWENTY
YOU ARE STRONGER THAN
YOU KNOW

"Be strong and courageous. Do not be afraid or discouraged. For the Lord your God is with you wherever you go."

JOSHUA 1:9 (NLT)

My cherished child,

Every time you step into the day without knowing how it will unfold, every time you show up with love, with integrity, with care - shows strength.

Every time you choose to keep going - that's courage.

It takes strength to keep showing up.

It takes courage to care.

It takes strength to let go of what you can't control. To speak gently when your emotions run deep. To hold space for someone else when your heart feels full.

It takes strength to keep saying yes to Me, one day at a time.

My Spirit lives within you.

You are stronger than you know.

I go before you into every battle, and I fight for you.

So, wherever you find yourself today, whatever is happening, however you feel - take courage. I am with you.

Let Me be your strength when you feel weak.

Let Me steady you, when you step into the unknown.

Let My grace carry you, when you think you can't take another step.

Let Me be your steady hand when the world around you feels fragile.

Let Me be your peace when the world feels overwhelming.

Let My presence calm your mind and bring you peace.

And wherever you go today - in small things and the big ones - remember, I am right there with you.

You are stronger than you think, and more loved than you could ever imagine.

So keep walking with Me. Keep showing up.

I'm right beside you - in each and every moment.

TWENTY-ONE
YOU ARE WONDERFULLY MADE

*"I praise you because I am fearfully and
wonderfully made; your works are
wonderful ...*

PSALM 139:14 (NIV)

Dear Daughter,

You are beautifully and wonderfully made - just as you are.

You are not a mistake. You are not random.

You are fully known, fully seen, and fully loved.

You are precious in My sight.

You are the apple of My eye.

I formed every part of you with intention.

Your voice, your strength, your presence - every part of you reflects My handiwork.

Your name is written on My heart, engraved on the palms of My hands.

You bring something to this world that no one else can offer.

I call you by name because I have redeemed you. You are My child. And I delight in who you are and who you are becoming.

Before you took your first breath, I loved you.

And My love is shaping you.

My love will never let you go.

Nothing in all creation can separate you from My love - not your past, not your fears, not your doubts, not even death itself.

I delight in every part of who you are and I love to hear your voice when you call to Me.

Come close to Me, exactly as you are.

Let this truth settle deep in your spirit today:

You are My beloved daughter.

You are perfectly made and perfectly loved, just as you are.

TWENTY-TWO
YOU ARE A LIFE-BRINGER

"The tongue can bring death or life; those who love to talk will reap the consequences."

PROVERBS 18:21 (NLT)

Dear Daughter,

When I spoke, the world was created with My word.

When I spoke, light broke through the darkness.

With My voice, I shaped oceans, stars, sky, and breath itself.

And because you are made in My image, your words carry creative power too.

You were created to be a voice of life, a bringer of light, and a speaker of truth in a dark world.

With your words, you can lift a heart, redirect a thought, or let someone know they are loved.

Your words can build and shape.

Your words can bring joy and hope.

Your words can bring healing.

Even your whisper, can speak My love.

Your words carry weight.

Your voice matters.

You are shaping hearts, and your voice is one of the tools I've given you to do it.

So let My love fill you.

Let My Words flow into you, and let your words overflow from that fullness.

Let My Spirit guide your thoughts, and let your words overflow from the life I've placed inside you.

Let your voice be a reflection of the grace and love you've received.

You were made to speak life, carry peace, and plant hope wherever you go.

So speak boldly, my daughter.

Speak gently.

Speak *life*.

TWENTY-THREE
YOU ARE SURROUNDED

*"Just as the mountains surround Jerusalem, so
the Lord surrounds his people, both now
and forever."*

PSALM 125:2 (NLT)

My Cherished Child,

My protection surrounds you - strong, constant, unbreakable.

I am with you, not just around you, but walking beside you, never leaving your side.

Even when you don't feel it, I am near.

I am all around you.

You are completely encircled by My care!

When you feel like the only one carrying the weight.

When questions echo quietly in your heart.

When the day stretches long and you're running on empty.

Remember this - My presence doesn't leave when things get hard.

My love doesn't give up on you.

My angels surround you - invisible guardians who stand watch and never sleep, never leave their post.

You are watched over, and gently upheld.

And all of heaven is with you.

Heaven's resources are at your disposal.

So take courage, my daughter.

You are not alone in this fight.

You are not forgotten.

The whole of heaven is leaning in, cheering you on.

You are seen, supported, and covered on every side.

You are being held more closely than you realize.

You are completely surrounded - by My presence, by My constant care, and by My unfailing love.

And I will never let you go.

TWENTY-FOUR
YOU ARE BUILDING SOMETHING ETERNAL

"Commit yourselves wholeheartedly to these commands that I am giving you today. Repeat them again and again to your children"

- DEUTERONOMY 6:6-7 (NLT)

My Beloved Daughter,

Each and every day you are building something eternal.

Not with bricks and stone - but with your quiet faith sown into each moment.

You may not always see it clearly, but what you're building will outlast you.

Each moment of kindness.

Each word of encouragement.

Each act of love.

Each quiet prayer.

You're sowing seeds that will bloom in hearts long after today is over.

You're shaping memories and forming values that will echo through generations.

Your legacy is not measured in perfect moments, but in faithful ones.

And in your love.

What you're building matters.

The love you give, the peace you carry, the words you speak - each of these are ordinary sacred moments.

So, stay close to Me.

Walk with Me.

Invite Me into your everyday rhythm.

Let Me fill your weary moments with My strength, your doubts with My wisdom, your impatience with My grace.

Keep going, beloved daughter.

What you're building will echo through generations.

And I am with you - in every ordinary, sacred moment.

TWENTY-FIVE
YOU ARE HELD THROUGH THE TEARS

"You keep track of all my sorrows. You have collected all my tears in your bottle. You have recorded each one in your book."

PSALM 56:8 (NLT)

My Precious Daughter,

When you come to Me, you don't have to pretend, or put on a good front.

You don't have to hold it all together.

It's okay to come to Me - just as you are. You are safe with Me.

I know the feelings you try to push aside - the quiet disappointments, the silent heartbreaks, the weight of being needed.

I see the tears you hide behind your smile. I hear the thoughts you've never said out loud.

Nothing that touches your heart escapes My notice. When your heart aches, I draw near. When your eyes fill with tears, I gather every one.

Bring them all to Me - every single one.

There's nothing too messy for Me to hold. Nothing's too much for Me to receive.

I long to carry those heavy burdens in your life.

You were never meant to carry it all on your own.

I am your safe place, your steady ground.

So don't hold back. Let the weariness speak.

Share your fears, your tears, your burdens with Me.

You are safe here with Me.

So let the tears fall.

Let Me hold what feels too much. Let Me carry what weighs you down.

I am there through every tear. Not one falls without My notice.

I gather each one and write it in My book.

Your tears matter to Me. You matter to Me.

And I am holding you, through every tear.

TWENTY-SIX
YOU ARE ANCHORED IN THE STORM

Therefore, we who have fled to him for refuge
can have great confidence as we hold to the
hope that lies before us. This hope is a strong
and trustworthy anchor for our souls.

HEBREWS 6:18-19 (NLT)

My Cherished Child,

Storms will come, and storms will pass—but they cannot shake My hold on you.

When the winds and waves rise, remember this: you are anchored in Me.

My love will keep you secure.

I will not let you go.

When questions crash like waves, pour your heart out to Me.

When the waters threaten to overwhelm, hold fast to My promises.

When fears rise in your heart, let Me carry you.

When your strength is failing, lean into Mine.

When the storm clouds threaten, turn to Me.

When the rain pours down, let Me be your shelter.

When the floods rise, let Me hold you up.

My truth can hold you steady.

For I will strengthen you. I will help you. I will keep you standing firm.

No storm can pull you from My hands.

No wave can wash you from My love.

I am your anchor, the steady ground beneath your feet.

With Me, you cannot be shaken.

So when the storm comes, remember—I am your anchor.

You are safe in Me.

And when the skies clear again, you will look back and see:

I was with you all along.

TWENTY-SEVEN
YOU ARE ENOUGH

"My grace is all you need. My power works best in weakness."

2 CORINTHIANS 12:9 (NLT)

My beautiful daughter,

I chose you before you took your first breath. I formed you with intention, with purpose, with delight.

My love for you isn't based on your performance.

You are already perfectly loved.

You don't have to prove your worth or earn your place at My table.

You are enough.

Just as you are.

So when the world makes its demands, remember who and whose you are.

You don't need to be everything to everyone.

Your strength comes from staying close to Me, because I am everything you need.

So, lay down the weight of endless doing.

Stop striving.

It's okay to rest.

Rest is not failure, or giving up.

Rest says, "I trust You more than I trust my own striving."

On those days when life feels heavy, let Me carry what you can't.

Give your burdens to Me.

Rest in Me.

Rest in My love.

I will take care of you.

You are Mine — and that is more than enough.

TWENTY-EIGHT

YOU ARE FORGIVEN AND FREE

"He is so rich in kindness and grace that He purchased our freedom with the blood of His Son and forgave our sins."

EPHESIANS 1:7 (NLT)

My precious child,

When the world tries to tell you otherwise, remember this - you are forgiven.

Completely. Freely. Forever.

You are free.

Because of My love, nothing stands between us now.

The price has already been paid in full - not by your effort, but by My love and mercy.

When I look at you, I don't see your past or your mistakes.

I see My grace at work in you. I see a heart made whole, a life set free.

My love is greater than any failure, deeper than any regret. Your debt has been cancelled.

You are no longer defined by what's behind you.

You are no longer a prisoner to what once held you back.

Your sins are gone - thrown into the depths of the sea, never to be held against you again.

You are defined by the One who goes before you and behind you.

So, when shame or guilt tries to cling to you, when regrets rise up, remember the truth of who you are.

You are forgiven. Set free.

Free from carrying the weight of your past, your pain, your burdens.

Free to rest in My grace and live in My love.

So lift your head, my daughter.

You have been redeemed.

You are My beloved daughter - restored and set apart for joy.

Let My truth speak to your heart.

Let My promises shape your future.

You are fully forgiven.

And gloriously free.

TWENTY-NINE
YOU ARE INVITED TO COME CLOSE

"My Presence will go with you, and I will give you rest."

EXODUS 33:14 (NLT)

My precious child,

Come. Step away from the noise and the busyness.

Lay aside the expectations, the lists, the things you've been carrying.

Just come - and be with Me.

Just for a minute.

Don't wait until everything is done.

Don't wait until you're running on empty.

I'm inviting you to stop *before* you run dry - to come and tell Me what's on your heart.

Come and listen.

Come and rest.

There is strength in the stillness.

You don't have to fill the silence - I'm already here.

I already know. I already care.

I long to spend time with you.

Let Me hold you.

Let Me remind you that you are already loved.

That you don't have to earn My love.

Who you are is enough.

This is your invitation, my dear one.

Come close.

Come before you're desperate.

Come because you're Mine.

Come and find the rest your soul craves.

Come as often as you need.

Come to where you belong - close to My heart, always.

THIRTY
YOU ARE CALLED BY NAME

*"Do not be afraid, for I have redeemed you. I
have called you by name; you are Mine."*

ISAIAH 43:1 (NLT)

Dear Daughter,

I know your name.

Your name is engraved on the palms of My hands.

I see you. You don't get lost in the crowd.

You are precious and honoured in My sight.

And I love you.

Before anyone else knew you, I did.

I formed you with care, called you with purpose, and chose you with joy.

I redeemed you. I called you by name.

You are Mine.

You are beloved, treasured, and set apart—not because of what you've done, but because of who I am, and who I made you to be.

I will never forget you—because you are My daughter.

And not just any daughter—you are a daughter of the King.

That title carries authority and promise.

When you feel small or insignificant, remember who and Whose you are.

Walk in the confidence of your royal heritage.

I call you to peace when fear rises. I call you to rest when you're weary.

I call you to courage, to joy, to stillness.

And always, I call you to Me.

You are never forgotten. You are known.

You are called by name—and you are Mine.

THIRTY-ONE

YOU ARE LOVED ALWAYS AND FOREVER

"I am convinced that nothing can ever separate us from God's love... nothing in all creation will ever be able to separate us from the love of God."

ROMANS 8:38–39 (NLT)

Dear Daughter,

You are loved - completely, constantly, unconditionally.

Not because of what you've done.

Not because of how well you've performed, how much you've given, or how strong you've stayed.

You are loved because you are Mine.

My love isn't based on how you feel or what the world says about you. It's anchored in who I am.

I have called you by name. I have written your name on My hands. And I love you.

There is nothing you can do to change that.

There is nothing anyone or anything else can do to change that.

My love is timeless, unending, and unshakeable.

So let your soul rest.

You are safe, wanted, chosen, and loved always.

I've been with you through every heartbreak, every triumph, every ordinary day.

Even in your hardest moments, this truth remains unchanged:

When you feel invisible or forgotten by the world - I love you.

When you question your worth or your purpose - I love you.

I love you.

Every moment of every day.

With every breath you take.

Always and forever.

AND FINALLY ....

You've made it to the end of this devotional — but really, it's only the beginning.

I hope that as you've turned these pages, you've felt *seen, known, and loved.*

Not because of anything you've done — but simply because of *who you are and whose you are.*

So, quiet your heart. *Lean in and listen for His voice.*

As you step into whatever's next, remember this:

You are already enough.

You are already loved.

And you are never too late for the plans God has for you.

AN INVITATION

Maybe as you've been reading these devotions, you've felt God's love tugging at your heart?

Perhaps you're wondering how to accept His invitation to become part of His family?

Here's the simple truth: God loves you so much that He sent His Son Jesus to bring you home.

The Bible tells us: *"God loved the world so much that he gave his only Son, so that everyone who believes in him will have eternal life and never be lost."* (John 3:16 MSG)

Just like you know your children's hearts, their fears, their dreams-God knows yours.

He sees the woman behind the roles, the dreams you've put on hold, the fears you carry.

And He loves every part of you.

You don't have to clean up your life first. You don't have to have it all figured out. God wants you just as you are, right now.

If you'd like to begin your own relationship with God and become His daughter forever, you can talk to Him right now.

Here's a simple prayer to help you:

Jesus,

Thank you for loving me just as I am.

I'm sorry for trying to do life on my own.

Thank you for dying for me and rising from the dead.

Please forgive me and make me new.

I invite you into my life-fill me with your Holy Spirit.

I choose to follow you today and always.

Amen

If you just prayed this prayer, welcome to God's family!

You are now His beloved daughter, and nothing can ever change that. Everything you've read about God's love for you is yours forever.

God's Holy Spirit now lives in you, giving you the strength to live this new life.

Your heavenly Father will be with you every step of the way as you begin this journey with Him.

What's Next?

Here are some simple ways to grow closer to God:

Tell a Christian friend or family member about your decision to follow Jesus

Start reading your Bible - you can get a physical Bible or download a Bible app

Find a church where you can make friends and learn more about God

Talk to God every day - just like you'd talk to a friend

God has beautiful plans for your life as you get to know Him better!

ONE MORE THING

If you've enjoyed this book, please consider leaving a rating or review. Thank you!

ABOUT THE AUTHOR

As a Christian woman who has lived through transition, loss, and the quiet wrestlings of motherhood, Evelyn Hope knows what it's like to wonder if God still has a purpose for you.

Her passion is to remind women that they are seen, loved, and still held by a faithful God - even when life feels uncertain.

You can find Evelyn's books on Amazon.

Loved Beyond Measure - a 3 minute daily devotional for teen girls, to help them understand their identity and immeasurable value to God.

www.ingramcontent.com/pod-product-compliance
Lightning Source LLC
Chambersburg PA
CBHW081251040426
42452CB00015B/2780